Nature vs. Technology –

Who's Winning?

Nature vs. Technology – Who's Winning?

D. J. Mathews

BookLocker

Trenton, Georgia

Print ISBN 978-1-959620-76-1
EBook ISBN: 979-8-88531-821-1

Published by BookLocker.com, Inc., Trenton, GA.

Health Disclaimer: The professional and health information provided is not meant to replace a doctor or other health professional when it comes to diagnosis of any health condition or illness.

Library of Congress Cataloging in Publication Data
MATHEWS, D. J. MATHEWS
NATURE VS. TECHNOLOGY – WHO'S WINNING?
Library of Congress Control Number: 2024916963

Booklocker.com, Inc.
2024

To

To sons Zeb, Adam, and Lincoln, and all the children of the future who will have to live with the effects of our technology, especially climate change.

DISCLAIMERS

This book provides content related to topics on physical and/or mental health issues. As such, use of this book implies your acceptance of the previous disclaimer.

Acknowledgements

Thanks for assistance from proofreader/editor Christina Levandowski. Thanks also to those allowing me to use their photos: Theodora Oniceanu for the big yellow truck under the name Theo Onic at Unsplash.com; Mitch Nielsen for the drone at Unsplash.com; The robot server, from the site freepik.com, with AI generation. Also, thanks to pxhere.com and creativecommons.org for the photo of the tree on fire.The cell phone girl was drawn by this writer. The Tower Bridge photo was taken by this writer and drawn on. And lastly, thanks to all the environmental organizations out there trying to make a difference.

Foreword

Here it is, folks, an eBook – yet another technological wonder. Mark Zuckerberg of Facebook fame has recently been encouraging us all to embrace the Metaverse and live in virtual reality, which his workers didn't even want to do. This thought prompts another: Our interest in such a virtual world "does" power this type of technology availability, *but is this really who we should be*?

Since the Industrial Revolution of the mid-1700s began, humans have become more and more dependent upon technology. Factories produced goods that were previously made slowly, by hand; horse drawn buggies then automobiles sped up the time it took to get us places.

Despite this momentum, we wanted more.

Since the late 1960s, we seemed to have made technological advances in hyper mode. We went to the moon, and we miniaturized computers till they could be carried around. (Howard Aiken, who helped design the 50 foot long Mark I computer, predicted this.) CAT scan machines made it easier to detect cancer or other body anomalies. We developed vaccines (at least in the case of the Covid-19 coronavirus) faster in order to deal with a pandemic. To top it off, the internet has made human interactions even faster and at greater distances.

After this summary on our advancements, I ask you to consider a few things:

Has nature, including human nature, kept up with all these advances, and are they beneficial overall? Have they caused more anxiety and stress in the modern age? Has technology pushed young people to consider suicide, or made it easier to commit murder? How did we survive without all these electronic devices in the past? Are they all necessary?

What about nature? How will Mother Nature survive, with CO2 emissions from human technology getting us closer and closer to the point of no return when it comes to the ill effects of climate change? Why, just the other day, a viewer in my area sent a picture of a funnel cloud developing before a heavy rain to the local TV station – and we're close to the East coast!

This little book will look at and answer some questions about whether nature (or human nature) is winning or really benefitting from all this technology, or is technology ruling the roost, to our detriment? We will look at the pros and cons, see which side is "winning," and more.

Table of Contents

Chapter One: The Internet: Important Tool Or the Bane of Our Existence? 1

Chapter Two: CARS – Helping or Hurting the Future? 7

Chapter Three: Good Food – A Necessity or a Luxury? 13

Chapter Four: The Ocean – Wondrous And Important To Us Every Day.. 19

Chapter Five: Space, the Final Frontier (Or Could We Say that about the Brain) 23

Chapter Six: Into the Wild Woods 27

Chapter Seven: Kids and Technology 31

Chapter Eight: Artificial Intelligence (A. I.) and Robots – Creepy or Essential?.. 35

Chapter Nine: Chemicals, Plastics (And What about the Ocean?) 41

Chapter Ten: Just a Few Words On the Pandemic............................. 47

Chapter Eleven: Meditation: A Break From Electronics 49

Chapter Twelve: Guns, Mass Shootings, Shot Deer (Oh My)............. 51

Chapter Thirteen: Climate Change.. 57

Chapter Fourteen: Conclusions (And Some Solutions) 61

Chapter Fifteen: Just a Few Updates... 71

(Most) References 73

Resources (Learn More/Join/Help out)... 75

About the Author 77

Chapter One:
The Internet: Important Tool
Or the Bane of Our Existence?

In a 1999 interview reported in the *Washington Post*, former Vice President Al Gore, running for president in 2000, said that he "created" the internet. That was an exaggeration, because he was not (publicly at least) a computer nerd, but someone who supported the U. S. Department of Defense's effort to expand the internet and its uses. (A stakeholder and enthusiast, if you will.)

Actually, in 1969 the U. S. Defense Department started to make the internet available, by putting it on the Department's online network. Working with the Advanced Research Projects Agency Network (ARPAnet) for a more secure way of communication, the Department needed the expertise of internet pioneer Vinton Cerf. Cerf actually had the assistance of Robert Kahn to create the procedures and protocol that would make the internet the formidable communication and knowledge spreading tool it would become. The National Science Foundation helped with a number of education and research connections. By 1989, it was spreading to common use for others, with the invention of the WorldWideWeb.

But Brit Sir Tim Berners- Lee, a computer scientist, is credited with inventing the World Wide Web itself. It was while working at CERN in Switzerland and researching "hypertext" that he created the World Wide Web, made available to all for free.

The internet, depending on one's point of view, has been the great uniter of people from far away. Or the great divider. A way for relatives and friends to stay in touch, or another method of communication that just creates arguments. Great encyclopedic-supported knowledge? Or crazy health, political, historical, or personal claims?

It depends on where you look.

This technological wonder, with a computer, <u>DSL</u> connection, and the like, allows you to put down your heartfelt thoughts (such as on Facebook and Twitter posts, a personal blog or <u>vlog</u>). Facebook has certainly had an influence on many people.

Facebook

Facebook is the "picture" site that has become so much more. Started by Mark Zuckerberg in 2003 (the name being changed from FaceMash to Facebook in 2004), it has surpassed the older "My Space" in use and popularity. People can post pictures of a trip, comment on a national issue, post silly cat videos, or even their own drawings.

Some have questioned whether putting all your personal information out in this virtual Wild West that is the internet is safe or appropriate. Little kids and where they can be found could be accessed by those online seeking to possibly kidnap them.

And when principals (at least in this writer's region) sought to hand out iPad tablets to middle school age children, did they realize there could be negative consequences to this new freedom? Many have learned to bypass adult safety protocols, to get on Facebook and other noneducational sites.

Cyberbullying, which involves harassment of students over the internet through various <u>social media</u> outlets, can cause students experiencing it to resort to drastic measures. These measures include refusing to go back to school, wanting education at home, and in some cases, committing suicide the trauma is so great. Sites like cyberbully.org have found that girls are as likely as boys to be bullied over the internet. Adolescents are quite impressionable and what is said online can lead to anger, frustration, low self-esteem, and thoughts of self-harm. This bullying can lead to behavior problems at school and even substance abuse.

This is such an issue that the Centers for Disease Control and Prevention (CDC) does a biennial survey on the issue of bullied students; since 2011 it has also researched electronic or cyberbullying. They use a <u>Youth Risk Behavior Surveillance System</u> for this. (These interesting surveys also monitor other behaviors like sexual activity, tobacco and vaping products use, and unstable housing conditions.)

In 2017, 15.5 percent of the students surveyed said they were cyberbullied; in 2013 it was 14.8 percent. Back in 2011 it was 16.2 percent of those surveyed; by 2019 (the last time data was available), it was 15.7 percent, so it is difficult to tell if it is increasing or decreasing substantially.

A few horror stories that parents have related, have out brought the issue of social media magnifying what bullying is already done in person at school. Ashlynn Conner was only ten when she took her own life. Why? At school they called her unkind names, like "ugly," and "fat," and also "slut," though the last word they probably didn't know the meaning of. She wanted to be homeschooled, but her mother refused. Social media use at home continued the verbal and mental abuse. She was found hanged in a home closet.

Kenneth Weishuln was 14 and had friends. Then he came out as gay and was bullied, even tormented by his old friends. He was harassed online and at school. He stopped it by committing suicide.

Social media can also cause harm to youth if a teen chats up a stranger online and offers to meet him, then is kidnapped. There are different dating type sites or apps (applications), from Eharmony to OkCupid. But when a young teen uses them, it can prove deadly.

One of the worse cases of dating apps proving deadly was the case of 13-year-old Virginian <u>Nicole Lovell</u>. Lovell had to have a liver transplant as a baby, and in doing so needed steroids to stay better, making her seem a bit overweight. She had a scar on her neck her peers made fun out and was miserable at school. Her parents watched her closely at home, but didn't realize she was totally unsupervised online. On her smartphone, she got this Kik dating app that allowed you to be anonymous. Through the app she met Virginia Tech athlete David Eisenhauer; she was lonely and communicated with him online for many hours. Eventually they met.

News reports later brought out that he had taken her to a party and had alcohol or used some other drug. He didn't remember what happened; Nicole informed him she might be pregnant. He was an 18 year old engineering student and the news shocked him. So he invited her to sneak out of her home one evening in 2016 for a "secret date" which turned deadly. He took her to a deserted road and stabbed her 14 times. In 2018 he was sentenced to 50 years in prison. Two young lives ruined by an online dating app. Sometimes dating sites can also lead to catfishing, defined as someone pretending to be somebody else. Many times this leads to the other person at the site being bilked out of thousands of dollars because the first person says he (usually he) desperately needs money. Be aware on these dating sites, and don't tell everything about yourself, like your home address and how much money you have in the bank.

There have some good uses for social interaction, of course. During the Covid-19, coronavirus pandemic, schools, churches, and businesses held classes online over the <u>Zoom</u> video conference service. And during the "Arab Spring" (from December 2010-2012) citizens in countries such as Yemen, Egypt, Syria, and more demonstrated for more rights and recorded it online for all to see. Many living in countries with oppressive regimes have found ways to connect with those in democracies through social media on the internet, giving them hope for a better life elsewhere, encouraging them to dream or take direct action to make it happen. You can have a better life elsewhere when you connect with others on this world wide web of possibilities, **if** you are careful.

But sometimes communication online can turn toward deadly deeds. The American Congress has recently listened to testimony gathered by the January 6ᵗʰ Commission about the January 6, 2021 insurrection at the U. S. Capitol building. Damning testimony has shown citizens listened to former President Donald Trump's advice to "march on the capitol" and protest election results, even though Joe Biden won the presidency fair and square, with more popular and electoral votes than Trump – there was no proof of widespread fraud to overturn the results.

Trump's December 19, 2020 tweet on Twitter/X to meet in D. C. January 6ᵗʰ, and be there because it "will be wild," encouraged thousands to show up. Thousands have since been arrested for literally breaking into the Capitol or trespassing, and threatening those who were verifying electoral count results to certify Biden as the next president. Several policemen died in this assault. It was not a good day for American democracy. Many online groups supporting that day have since been investigated for their part in inciting this violent protest. Some believe this has given a black eye to America's image in the world.

So, the internet has many pros and cons. Do we keep this mechanism for great communication and knowledge? Perhaps some laws regulating political incitement, dating apps, and racist speech are in order. When it comes to the nature vs. technology argument, some negative aspects of the internet are winning. But people are looking more at regulation, so neither side wins this one.

Chapter Two:
CARS – Helping or Hurting the Future?

We Americans and most Western countries it seems, have this all consuming love affair with the family car. When I taught at a university, I noticed most students brought their own cars. I asked myself – really? Even when the campus isn't a full block away from a pizza place, clothing store, or bank? Doesn't anyone believe in walking anymore?

Henry Ford probably never conceived of there being millions and millions of cars, trucks, and SUVs (sports utility vehicles) on major highways like our interstate system (started in 1956, thanks to President Dwight Eisenhower) when he began the automobile assembly line in 1913. But face it. We love our cars. They take us to national parks, Grandma's house for the holidays, fancy restaurants, work, and beaches. Even college dorms, rest homes, and apartments. We just plain "need" these electronic horses, right?

But can we keep this wondrous convenience going in the future? Will we ever run out of parts? Maybe not, but what about if fueling them becomes an issue, an existential crisis for some (environmentalists)? Is this the best option for our planet?

Looking back, fossil fuels have been around since the late 1800s, when electric batteries were not perfected enough to overtake gasoline as the fuel of choice for the automobile/car. Coal was also being dug around that time, but the combustion engine, using gasoline, became popular and took off.

Then came air pollution, CO2 emissions, smog. The average passenger vehicle in the U.S. emits 4.6 metric tons (!) of carbon dioxide a year. According to the Union of Concerned Scientists, our trucks, cars, planes, trains, freight, and shipping produce nearly 30 percent of

U. S. global warming emissions. And global warming or climate change, is creating more and stronger storms, churning up our oceans into a frenzy of activity no one wants to deal with, it seems. Some, though, are taking the lead in efforts to reduce vehicle emissions.

Billionaire Elon Musk, who founded the Tesla car company in 2003, is one of the few multi-millionaires out there promoting sustainability on the planet through electric powered vehicles. Electric cars are becoming more and more a part of the American market, with hybrids (part-electric, part-gas powered) also contributing toward lowering the amount of CO2 emissions in the air. Extremely ambitious and motivated, Musk has also cofounded (then sold) PayPal, been a lead designer at SpaceX for rocket and spaceship development, and has home solar energy storage batteries called "Powerwall" available to the public now. Though he may have issues with Twitter/X ownership, Musk has said that overall, he wants to do "useful things for civilization."

Is this enough to reverse the ill effects of climate change (and you do know fossil fuels will eventually run out)? Good question. But interest in clean air has grown, along with government mandates for car manufacturers to improve fuel efficiency on the highway, meaning more miles with less gas used. Electric and hybrid cars "can" make a difference when it comes to lowering carbon dioxide emissions.

It may be surprising to know that cars started out being hand cranked. Now you don't need that – batteries used with internal combustion engines power things like the radio and air conditioning, work the starter, get the crank shaft moving initially so that something can "combust" to begin with. An all-electric car doesn't need the combustion part of the equation, though a hybrid car does.

With cars during these inflationary times using gas costing up to $4.00+ a gallon, it is no wonder manufacturers and citizens both are gravitating toward electric vehicles. Even the Volkswagen and Hyundai brands and the Ford mustang (the 2023 Mach-E) have EV models.

Currently (as this is being published), there are three types of fuel efficient vehicles putting out little to no CO2 emissions. There is the Hybrid Electric (HEV), the Plug-in Hybrid Electric Vehicle (PHEV), and the Battery Electric car (BEV). The <u>HEV</u> vehicle has gasoline kick in as it brakes, especially when standing at a stoplight. This "regenerative" braking can help recharge the car. It can cruise along at low speeds after reaching a certain threshold, during which the gasoline part then kicks in (according to ConservationInstitute.org).

There is also a Honda hybrid out there and the Toyota Prius, the Prius at a little over $27,000 in 2024. The Toyota Corolla Hybrid is even cheaper, at $23,500. (See more info at <u>https://cars.usnews.com/cars-trucks/toyota/prius</u> .)

According to a recent *AARP* newsletter, in 2022, buying EVs now qualifies for a federal tax credit, up to $7,500. (See <u>https://afdc.energy.gov/laws/state</u> .) Credits vary, according to the brand of car. (Go to <u>https://www.nerdwallet.com/article/taxes/ev-tax-credit-electric-vehicle-tax-credit</u>.)

The latest government stats are very encouraging. The new EV cars tend to average around 250 miles on a single, full charge. The 2022 Ford F-150 Lightning 4WD Extended Range (A1) can get 73 MPGe in the city, 66 MPGe on the highway. (MPGe means miles per gallon equivalent.) The 2024 Hyundai Kona Electric can do even better, with an EPA estimated range of up to 261 miles. Impressive.

These seem to be economical choices (after you get over the sticker shock – electric cars usually cost $27,000 to $100,000, hybrids over $25,000). But are they worthwhile in the long term for the planet? After all, you have to mostly "plug-in" to get the electricity for the vehicle, and most electricity in the U. S. still depends on fossil fuels (22 percent from coal and 38 percent from natural gas in 2021), both polluting the air. Perhaps we could do Iceland's experiment with hydrogen power for buses in the future.

You know what is also economical? Riding a bike to work. This writer knew a young doctor who used to cycle to his job at a local emergency room. Not practical for everyone, but if you are in good shape and traffic patterns allow in bikers with special lanes, it's an option. Using transportation already there – such as trains, subways, buses – is another way to use less gasoline and pollute the air less. There is also the idea of riding to work with someone, or waiting till Friday or Saturday to do nearby errands altogether. For more options, see https://sharetheride.com/#/.

Another thing that is not fully developed – self driving cars. China's been using them in public transport, but if something is already on a track, that makes it a whole lot easier than being in a car on the interstate or in downtown traffic. Some of us would love to do a puzzle, read the paper, or watch a movie as the car rolls on, letting "Mr. Car" do the rest. Tesla's electric cars are working on an advanced driver assistance system (ADAS), an article in *Reader's Digest* points out. Yet it is only on Level 2 of a five stage system of automation.

We're definitely not there yet. But don't most of us want control of our own cars, as there are too many accidents on the road a year in this country now? But one older couple interviewed in Arizona felt being in a self-driving car was great and so have others. (See https://www.wbur.org/hereandnow/2021/01/04/waymo-driverless-car.) Still, there have been accidents with this new innovation, and no one has talked about the many *Lyft* and *Uber* drivers who'd be replaced – what would they do next?

And forget about flying cars! From imaginary highways in the *Back to the Future* movies and TV's "The Jetsons," flying cars are kind of, yeah, impractical. Although The Jetsons did predict some things we use now, like video calls, holograms, jet packs (for astronauts at least), we don't currently have robotic maids. Inventors working on a part jet, part car vehicle estimate it costing over $100,00 to produce. And where would your "highway" be? We've barely been regulating other flying objects like drones, especially the little ones being used for some delivery services, like the new <u>Wing</u> service in Christiansburg, Virginia. Flying cars may just be too tricky to manage.

All these innovations use resources. Hybrid EV cars especially, need a sizable lithium battery in order to operate. Unfortunately, lithium is not very renewable at this point. Lithium is an odd chemical. It floats in water. You can cut it with a knife, but it is also highly reactive, an alkali metal that's been around for eons. It is not easy to mine, so it is costly. There is a lot in South American salt deserts, and can even be found in seawater. Researchers are working diligently with the seawater to create an electro-chemical battery. And the ocean has five times more of the element than land does.

Like a lot of processes, it needs a bunch of water. We can get it from other places, like Argentina, Chile, Bolivia, China, the South American countries, with over 50 percent of the world's lithium. We presently own only one mine in Nevada for this alkali metal.

So where will the supply for lithium be in 10 years? Will it be difficult to produce (then become as expensive or even more so than oil is today)? Can we make a battery that can self-recharge at some point? We may need to turn to the possibility of a hydrogen cell for renewable car energy sometime in the future.

Since most of us don't live close to our jobs, vehicles provide a beneficial technology overall, currently a win for people.

Chapter Three:
Good Food – A Necessity or a Luxury?

Food. Here in abundant America, it's everywhere, such as the local gas station, supermarket, restaurant, or laundromat. We're definitely not Ethiopia, Sudan, parts of Central America where many are starving to eat (literally). In some big cities, though, the U. S. does have food deserts or a lack of a grocery store to easily get to. *Feeding America* now says in Virginia alone, 658,470 people are facing hunger, with over 182,000 of them kids. (But that's a topic for another book.)

In America, even with just a few dollars in your pocket, you can buy a candy bar and hamburger. Yes, we have a lot of fast food joints, Chinese takeout, chips you can get at a gas station and gobble up in the car on the way to your next destination. Our attitude toward food is decidedly cavalier. Any food will do, any hamburger, carrot, chocolate bar, smoothie, etc.

Is all our food and what's in it healthy? Why are we so obsessed with sugar (this writer included)? Refining sugar and using it have been around since about 4,000 B. C. And it didn't come from the Americas originally, but Southeast Asia, Papua New Guinea being the oldest place of origin. But when the "East Indies" Company went to, well, the East Indies in the 16th century or so, sugar came from India, a great place of interest. Even before that the West Indies or Caribbean was growing the stuff, helping, unfortunately, to contribute to the slave trade.

And it's been with us ever since.

It also seems to be in everything we eat. Yes, some form of sugar is in that adorable, spongy *Twinkie* cake or soda pop. It's also in unlikely sources like spaghetti sauce, cereal, soups, ketchup, or salad dressing. No wonder so many of us crave sweets.

What about soda?

Soda pop or just soda (so-called because it has "some" sodium in it) has been around a while. A carbonated mineral water was created in 1783. Then came *Hires Root Beer* (1876), *Dr. Pepper* (1885), *Coca-Cola* (1886), and *Pepsi* (1893). *Vernors' Ginger Ale* is considered the oldest though.
(See https://www.rfdtv.com/the-oldest-soda-pop-in-america-belongs-to-vernors.)

So, these "soft drinks" (as opposed to hard drinks which contain alcohol) have actually been here longer than you think. In 1767 Joseph Priestley, an English chemist, along with others in Europe, came up with the idea of carbonation, or adding carbon dioxide to soft drinks, which gives soda a bit of a kick. Even **more of a kick** was when the Coca-Cola Company actually put some cocaine in its drink, apparently as a pick-me-up. It was not illegal in the 1880s and was not a major ingredient, if you believe the history about it. Inventor John Pemberton actually called Coke a "brain tonic." Really?

Mostly, that **is** what soda is – a pick-me-up. It has no protein, vitamins, or minerals. The sweetener in soda, be it aspartame, cane sugar, or corn syrup, is not good for you. The February 2001 issue of the journal *Lancet* said that in an independent study, it was learned that sweetened beverages increased the obesity rate in kids. For every can of soda a child drinks a day, the odds of becoming obese rise 60 percent.

Additives to soda may not be all that healthy either. ActiveBeat.com points up the fact that the artificial sweetener aspartame has been linked to allergic reactions and headaches. The FDA (Food and Drug Administration) has even found a link between it and possibly a decrease in insulin sensitivity. Whether it is carcinogenic has been debated by the FDA and WHO (World Health Organization). (But do you want to take that chance?)

Actually, the International Agency for Research on Cancer (IARC) says aspartame is a "possible carcinogen" now.

Moreover, other researchers have found drinking two or more sodas a week almost doubles a person's risk of developing pancreatic cancer. There were 60,524 participants in a particular Singapore-Chinese (14 year study), yielding 140 cases of pancreatic cancer. It's also been found that pancreatic carcinoma is related to past habitual intake of total carbohydrates and simple sugar consumption. What are healthier drinks? Lowfat organic milk, teas, coffee without all those toppings at *Starbucks*, or filtered water.

Additives to food *can* cause problems, then. You need to watch out.

GMOs (Oh My)

What about GMOs – genetically modified organisms, basically foods with genes that have been manipulated in the laboratory to bring better results to consumers? We're talking corn, soy, and possibly wheat, the last the U. S. FDA approved for use in 2023. The *Business Insider* points out potatoes, apples, and even Canola oil and summer squash (zucchini) are GMO now, in a process that began in 1994.

Has there been any long term research to prove GMO food is safe?

People worry about food allergies and metabolism effects, says Claire Muszalski, a registered dietician with the University of Pittsburgh Medical Center. Presently, nine out of 10 members of the American Association for the Advancement of Science think they are "generally safe." By the end of 2022, the USDA required labeling of grocery products if they had been bioengineered, and say "bioengineered" on the label.

GMO corn produces toxins that are toxic to certain bugs, not considered harmful to humans and livestock. Also, there are GMO soybeans in everything, seemingly replacing corn syrup, as well as GMO canola oil, sugar beets, potatoes, papaya, apples.

And at the same time, GMO crops have led to rampant use of pesticides.

What is worrisome are these pesticides, put **on the plants** as they grow. *Roundup*, made by Monsanto, contains glyphosate and is sprayed on some plants prior to harvest for an "efficient" harvesting technique called desiccation.

In 2015, a WHO report identified glyphosate as a probable human carcinogen. (Maybe you have seen commercials advertising lawyers ready to go to court over those with Non-Hodgin's lymphoma because of glyphosate exposure.) EU countries have banned this pesticide's use. Consumers may have to decide for themselves which foods are healthiest to eat that are not organic. See this site for more info on organic labels and processes: https://www.mayoclinic.org/healthy-lifestyle/nutrition-and-healthy-eating/in-depth/organic-food/art-20043880.

Regenerative Agriculture

For several years this writer taught a class on logic and writing. In one of those classes the theme was food – the good, the bad, and in-between. We read part of Michael Pollan's *The Omnivore's Dilemma,* and saw the film *Food, Inc.* The movie was especially poignant because it pointed up the fact that the meat industry has shrunk to only a handful of producers. It's a real **assembly line of farming** we've got going now.

Cows "naturally" eat grasses that their one stomach (with four different compartments) breaks down. (Aside – did you know that when a cow is chewing her "cud" she's eating partly digested food she has thrown up? Disgusting.)

But our fast, assembly line production of beef-to-eat doesn't allow for much of that. Beef cattle are fed mostly corn to fatten up at so called feedlots, where they are mostly standing and eating. When they are slaughtered, they are actually starting to get sick on all that danged corn, not natural for their systems. Yeah, and our hamburgers come from that. Organic, grass fed beef is generally rather expensive though.

More farmers, though, are turning back to the "old ways" of farming, a more natural, regenerative approach for the entire farm environment. There is the use of animal manure instead of manmade, synthetic fertilizer. Cows go from field to field to graze and eat, working to create healthy soil in the process, which can draw down carbon dioxide. There is also the natural use of pest control like ladybugs (not *Roundup*).

People with their own backyard gardens can explore more natural, organic gardening methods. (This gardener does **NOT** use the insecticide *Sevin*, for example). On NPR (National Public Radio) Mike McGrath, for years, has given tips on organic gardening on his *You Bet Your Garden* show *(*See *https://www.wlvt.org/television/you-bet-your-garden/.)*

For farmers not yet convinced of the benefits of natural/organic farming, there is the <u>Soil Carbon Initiative</u> (SCI). The SCI would help you by providing a third party and independent verification of these regenerative agriculture outcomes. Issues addressed would include biodiversity, improved water use and quality, and rural prosperity. And, of course, carbon dioxide reduction. And that beats the feedlot and present monoculture/ industrial production methods of growing the same crops over and over in the same ol' place, <u>reducing the nutrients</u> in grocery store vegetables quite a bit.

One last thought is from farmer/teacher/author <u>Wendell Berry</u>. He writes about a lack of connection to the land in *The Unsettling of America*. He believes we've become a nation of specialists. Specialization, whether it is being an education specialist who doesn't teach, or inventors of devices with no concern for the effects of these devices (like "living" on the iPhone), has Americans consigning food production to agribusiness.

Berry believes all this specialization separates us and doesn't create community. A farmer should be seen as a nurturer, he says, not a businessman. We should be growing more of our own food, teaching kids to plant vegetables, tending toward organic, avoiding refined sugar. That would be a start toward control of our health, at least. In the nature vs. technology argument, technology has somewhat dominated the farming arena. Some find this an unhealthy situation.

Chapter Four:
The Ocean – Wondrous And
Important To Us Every Day

As a kid growing up on Long Island (NY), sometimes my family and I visited the renown <u>Jones Beach</u>. I remember the greenish-blue water and waves rapidly breaking over us on hot summer days. The last time I visited, as an adult, the water was surprisingly cold.

Of course, this New York attraction was cold. It's part of the ocean, after all, that huge body of water covering 71 percent of the earth's surface. But being saltwater, we can't really drink it.

Environmental writer Rachel Carson felt it was so special she wrote a book about it, *The Sea Around Us*. A National Book Award winner in 1952, her book looks at the history of the earth and sea, of nonstop rains and giant squids battling sperm whales, and a recent addition to the book now looks at the fragility of life with our dying coral reefs, and how oil spills and pollution hurt these waters.

As Carson previously pointed out, the ocean is a special world all by itself. If you were caught under a wave and happened to swallow some seawater, you'd be swallowing some salty water, but also algae, fish larvae, sea snails (possibly), and jellyfish. Phytoplankton are actually microscopic algae or plants (although some phytoplankton include bacteria or protists or single celled protozoan or alga). Most of them can be involved with photosynthesis, with the byproduct of oxygen. The word "plankton" comes from the Greek, "to wander or drift," and these drifters actually produce much of the oxygen we breathe, 50-80 percent, depending on whose <u>research</u> you go by.

Phytoplankton is also food for zooplankton, tiny animals in the sea. The phytoplankton is really small. How small can phytoplankton be? Really tiny. Just how tiny is tiny? Tiny is one to 1,000 micrometers or microns, and a micron is 0.001 mm, or a thousandth of a millimeter. And 25 millimeters = an inch. Yes, tiny enough for something almost as tiny to consume it.

Algae and micro algae have been used in skincare and cosmetics for centuries, their chlorophyll, vitamin E, and <u>ectoine</u> used to protect against free radical damage and UV rays. There is also <u>research</u> being done on using coral reefs' bacteria residents, for treating cancer.

Interesting creatures lurking in the ocean include colorful sea slugs, and the 196 ton blue whale, so called because of its mottled, blue gray color. It depends on tiny beings, shrimplike critters called krill. It seeks out krill with the baleen hairs connected to its upper jaw –look, ma, no teeth!

Another unique creature is the tiny immortal jellyfish (Turritopsis dohrnii). It begins life as a larva, called a planula. It swims for a while, then attaches to the sea floor, and grows into a colony of polyps, which in turn spawn identical medusae or jellyfish.

Full grown, the Turritopsis dohrnii is only 4.5 mm or .18 inches across, smaller than a pinky nail. Yet, it has 90 white, tiny, tiny tentacles it moves about with. But if it is damaged or starved, it can transform itself back to a polyp rooted to the sea floor again.

This is remarkable. This process is called "transdifferentiation". Scientists are thinking, hey, why not study this unique way of cell recycling? Could we possibly regenerate human stem cells or a human heart damaged by disease? It's an idea! (Few of us, though, would probably want to live forever.) The immortal jellyfish is also good at hitchhiking onto ships in the ballast water and surviving long journeys at sea.

There was a show on the *Netflix* streaming channel/app called "My Octopus Teacher," about a swimmer in a South African kelp forest who develops a relationship with an octopus. It was kind of like approaching an alien being. He touched and connected with the little reddish brown cephalopod. He felt she taught him how to be a part of the ocean, to be vulnerable, to connect more with people, and the ocean too.

They say the octopus is quite intelligent. It will try to escape from an aquarium. It has a ton of neurons, giving it "brains" in each of its independently moving eight legs, working separately from its central brain. The head is weird, with an esophagus running through that central brain. So, if it swallowed a sharp object, would it be bye-bye cephalopod? This writer has also read that the Korean people will try to eat a live octopus tentacle. It can sometimes choke the person trying to eat it, to death, with human and tentacle both dying. So regular fish aren't wild enough for you?

Our ocean is full of wondrous water animals, produces oxygen we need to breathe, has fish we can eat, if we don't overfish its populations. It deserves our attention and protection.

Dang it, it must be mentioned, that elephant in the room – rising seas due to climate change causing glaciers to melt into the sea and threatening coastal cities and Pacific islands too. Some coastal cities, at least, are doing something to mitigate the situation.

New Orleans, on the U. S. coastline and touching the Gulf of Mexico, is sinking. According to <u>NOLA.com</u>, the French settled the city 300 years ago on a natural high point, with marsh and swamp beyond it. Over the years the land has been drained, compacted, and now is sinking. So, the city needs to regroup and change. There are now plans to rebuild levees (embankments to prevent flooding) and even use pump stations for flooding areas. Plus, the city plans to raise buildings themselves to help floodproof them.

As for our most populous city in America, New York City, the Statue of Liberty has toes 154 feet above the harbor. It is predicted they won't get wet till 2100. Why? It's because N. Y. City is also sinking. (In the past glaciers have caused land to bulge as it is being pressed down.)

So, we need the ocean. It can be a "win-win" for us humans if we take better care of it. But we don't need it in our backyard, do we? If you live on the coast, it would be a good idea to move uphill or get some house stilts.

Chapter Five:
Space, the Final Frontier (Or Could
We Say that about the Brain)

"Space... the final frontier. These are the voyages of the Starship Enterprise...." Thus began a very imaginative American television series whose ideas have continued well past its beginning in 1966, when *Star Trek* the original series first aired on TV.

It was the imaginative concept of Gene Roddenberry, a former pilot and policeman and writer, who projected into the distant future, some 200 years from now, when people would fly to other planets and galaxies at warp speed (the speed of light or faster) to meet with alien beings. They were mostly humanlike in appearance, with eyes, a mouth, walking limbs, something like hands, and in colorful costumes to remind us aliens have a lousy fashion sense.

Many times, they were more warlike than peaceful, and not too cute – except for those furry round Tribbles, who the doctor known as "Bones" surmised were born pregnant so reproduction was almost instant. What can you say about this? This is great science fiction for sure.

But is **everything** about the Star Trek TV shows and movies just a dream and impossible?

About the Future

Movie character Marty McFly wants to tell you "about the future," though we can't yet drive to the past at 88 miles per hour. That would be unrealistic. Is anything in the Star Trek series realistic concerning future space travel and human life experiences?

Like food replicators. Would that ever be possible? If you are in space millions of miles from earth, there would logically be no grocery store out there with fresh food to eat. In the *Star Trek: Enterprise* series (with actors Scott Bakula and Jolene Blalock), Bakula as Capt. Archer mentions that "Chef" will make meals, and they always look supermarket ready. It's more likely meals, like those eaten up at the International Space Station 250 miles (400 kilometers) above sea level, would be from those vacuum-packed MREs (Meals Ready to Eat), like our military uses.

But can a steak, mostly protein, be made with some kind of replicator machine?

Researchers have worked to build chains and layers of amino acids and proteins, almost in 3D fashion. But this would take "tons" of work, and wouldn't really taste much like steak. And it would cost, like, $330,000 dollars to make, based on an experiment done in Europe.

Mark Post's team at Maastricht University in the Netherlands worked for months to create a hamburger in petri dishes, but it didn't taste like much. (No fat or salt added.) Could this be practiced on a spaceship far away? Maybe, if the process were perfected to taste better and cost less.

What about warp speed (traveling at the speed of light)? If a spaceship "could" approach warp speed, then in no time at all you'd be examining what life there is (or isn't) near the nearest star, Alpha Centauri (which is actually part of a three star system around four light years away). You could probably survive on those MREs for a while, and if you had a place for frozen vegetables or could plant potatoes, like actor Matt Damon did in that Mars movie, with a hydroponic system of some kind, you wouldn't starve – not unless there was **really** no life there, or plants you could grow food from once you arrived.

As for actually traveling superfast through space, there are some theories about whether something approaching warp drive could be achieved. Scientist Erik Lentz has a theory that would use conventional physics, not the matter-anti-matter machine used in Star Trek adventures. This <u>Alcubierre Drive</u> would somehow contract and twist space using negative energy, putting your ship in a kind of bubble where you don't discern the great speed you are traveling at. But it would require tons of energy, a theoretical idea at this point.

For now, we have visionaries (or whatever you want to call them), like Elon Musk, urging us to prepare for life on Mars.

Our first astronauts flew to and explored the moon, which looks pretty close in the night sky. NASA says it is 238, 855 miles away, the equivalent of 30 earths, which doesn't seem possible. But space is so supremely vast, so spacious, if you will. Traveling to Mars at today's speeds would take several months, easy. According to NASA a one way trip to Mars would take nine months, and 21 months for a round trip because you would need for the earth and Mars to be in a suitable location for the trip back.

Musk is projecting there could be a colony on Mars, possibly built into a cave, by 2060. This is conjecture, of course. We don't even have a colony on the moon yet, a good training ground for space travel somewhere else. But we do have astronauts planning to fly "around" the moon in the near future. It's a start.

For now, we have the <u>James Webb Space Telescope</u>, replacing the aging Hubble Telescope as the go-to technology to show us the universe millions and millions of miles away. It can snap infrared photos of beginning stars that are highly detailed. The Hubble is only 570 kilometers from earth. The Webb Telescope is 1.5 million kilometers (almost a million miles) away. The gravitational pull of both the sun and earth keep it in earth's orbit, a fantastic feat of physics. It is hoped the telescope could look back in time, getting us very close – like 100 million years – to the beginnings of life, close to the Big Bang itself.

Space travel so far has given us technologies we can use right here on earth, like Velcro, and CAT machine and MRIs used in medicine. Also, the drink "Tang" and even the digital imaging breast biopsy system. In the future, if earth becomes unlivable because of climate change, we may **have to** depend on what is out there, out in the darkness, where there are many other worlds to explore. Outer space technology could certainly provide us a helpful support system, a definite pro for people.

Chapter Six:
Into the Wild Woods

Have you met Mother Nature? She gives us sunny days and green gardens, calm, crystal clear, bluish waters, and trees half a mile high – well, they're not "really" that tall. They just look like they touch the sky, an example being trees like the coastal California redwood, growing to 367 feet tall (112 meters).

Mother Nature also gives us punishing environments – brutal winds almost shouting down Emperor penguins guarding eggs on Antarctica's snow, and other environments where it's hard to find any food to live on.

Environments without food don't include your city Kroger supermarket. We're talking way up in Alaska and Canada. On the reality TV show contest *Alone*, this *History Channel* show gives us a fascinating example of what people did "without," before current technology, maybe 200 years ago. That was before there were heat pumps and air conditioning, TVs and super shopping centers, and in some cases, guns, when people had to use ingenuity to survive on the land. You used an axe, a small saw to cut down slim trees and tree boughs to create a small shelter. Flint or sharp stones helped start a fire with kindling (tiny twigs, dry moss), and most of the ten participants in this TV show have maybe one knife, one pot, one sleeping bag, without a pillow. It's just the basics the first settlers had.

If it's winter or almost winter, food is hard to come by. You put a little wire snare out in the woods hoping for a bunny to get caught in it, or you put your <u>gill net</u> in the cold yet turquoise hued lake to try to catch a fish. Or employ a bow and arrow to shoot bigger game. And then miss that duck/deer/mountain lion/ (fill in the blank).

These are men and a few women trying to "really" get in touch with nature, with no outside help. And man, it's not easy, yet so interesting to watch. Most of these participants are under age 40, talk to a camera they lug around with them as they explore the woods and water in a region (for most of the shows) in upper Canada, as they try to out-survive each other for the $500,000 prize. Woo!

Some have lasted three months in a region just below the Artic Circle. There is no way *this* writer could last that long, probably putting together a crummy shelter (have weak wrists) and having trouble keeping a fire going at night.

In one episode a guy, the fourth one left, stirred up his fire. His ceiling of wood and pine boughs caught fire. He stood outside his dwelling all night and watched it burn down. Then he used his satellite phone, one of a few technology assists allowed, to "tap out" of the contest, his domicile destroyed in a snowy, early winter scene backdrop.

Another famous or infamous mishap with man against nature adventure was that of Christopher McCandless. He tried to go all "Jack London" (the author of books *White Fang* and *Call of the Wild*) in the early 1990s. It was before there were widespread cell phones and GPS devices, or even a phone booth nearby he knew about. He probably didn't even have a compass. Without giving his family his exact location, McCandless set off for Alaska, arrived, and after some time there wanted to go home. He got a bit lost and couldn't get across the Teklanika River in central Alaska. He holed up in an old bus hunters had used and couldn't get enough to eat in the wilderness.

Unlike the *Alone* contestants who have camera crews and a doctor to check up on them before they lose too much weight, McCandless had no one to check up on him and starved to death. Jon Krakauer, author of the book about this young man, *Into The Wild*, now has some scientific proof that McCandless, who lost half his body weight when found (according to his driver's license), starved because he ate wild potato seeds that contained a chemical that would make him too weak to get up and look for food, basically <u>ODAP poisoning</u>. If you don't positively know what you are doing and you are in the middle of nowhere with no way to reach people, Mother Nature can be deadly.

But it needs to be added that you don't have to hike "to the middle of nowhere" in Alaska in order to be alone. Sometimes being alone is just taking a stroll in your neighborhood at dinnertime, around 5-6 p.m. Or renting a canoe to take on a nearby river. The "wild" is a whole lot closer than you think.

Some helpful tips for surviving in the wild (like if you get lost on a hike or shipwrecked) can be found in Les Stroud's book *Survive! Essential Skills and Tactics to Get You Out of Anywhere – Alive*. He optimistically states that you could survive a month in the wild without food, but there **are** many food sources in the wild if you know where to look, and it's not the middle of winter. Many early explorers, in fact, died from scurvy, not knowing that the spruce boughs they slept on in the wild they could have made into a tea to give them the vitamin C they needed. There are mushrooms and berries out there, but you really need a guidebook and some training to properly I. D. them.

If you know how to use kindling like twigs, moss, or dry leaves and click together sharp stones and start a fire, you could roast grasshoppers, crickets, worms – better than nothing. Violet flowers and leaves are edible without cooking, as are garlic mustard, goosefoot, many other plants, but again, a guidebook is needed if you didn't grow up eating them. This includes wild blackberries, raspberries, wineberries, or blueberries in season.

You can crack open the hard outer skin of an acorn for the bitter meat inside, or eat the inner, celerylike shaft of a cattail stem or suck on pine needles or make them into a broth, if need be. It is best to know what to do in an emergency **before** you are left out in the middle of nowhere, because without some kind of technology, Mother Nature rules the day and wins, hands down.

Chapter Seven:
Kids and Technology

You just **knew** this was going to be talked about again, right?

Yes, let's have a bit more of a discussion concerning kids and today's technology. We've already mentioned how all this interest in technological devices is making kids sit around the house and get FAT. And young, naïve teens on dating apps can be put in potentially dangerous situations.

This writer was concerned when, living in a rural community with few recreational possibilities, our sons spent a fair amount of time playing video games – mostly the less violent <u>RPG</u> kind. Technology use for information and entertainment among kids and teens has risen exponentially, with even <u>eight year olds</u> on devices a lot, according to the *New York Times*.

Even two "educated" parents may stick their kids in front of a TV or smaller electronic device so they can clean the house or get dinner ready to serve on the table. What to do, what to do about this?

It is a quandary for some busy parents or guardians, or the lone grandmother who hasn't the energy to constantly distract a child. (Putting a child outside in the yard and/or getting them to play a game with a peer can help. Sometimes you just have to ask others in your community for help. Let's get out the coloring book and art pad.)

Cell Phone Use In School

In an op-ed originally appearing in the *Chicago Tribune*, ninth grade English teacher Liz Shulman expressed great concern for her students, because they seemed so distracted yet also "attracted" to phone apps (applications). She pointed out schools may require cell phones in class to be collected, or the teacher may offer extra credit or even candy to put them away. They recognize that these kids are kind of addicted, and even have **clueless parents** constantly texting them when they should be paying attention to learn something instead.

Shulman further argued that a 2018 Pew Research Center report disclosed that 54 percent of teens admitted they spent too much time on their phones. And 60 percent admitted this was a big problem for them.

In the past, students threw spit wads and passed notes or hid comic books inside their textbooks for a distraction. But that didn't keep them from learning their subjects in class. Logically, in school students should be able to debate and be exposed to new ideas, without so many distractions.

Continuing this attachment to the internet can have consequences. Sociologist and writer Sherry Turkle interviewed a student named Trevor in 2009. He felt conversation had "died" once his generation discovered Facebook. By the time they graduated college he found people would eat together but be quiet and on their phones. He even felt going out for a drink felt like "too much work." How many other young adults feel this way?

Turkle also discovered that in an upper middle class middle school in upstate New York, students found it difficult to read and understand facial expressions, or have much empathy for their peers. Some younger than that could develop "text neck" from looking down at their phones.

There is actually a parents' group out there that feels kids should "wait till 8th grade" to get a smartphone (<u>waittill8th.org</u>). Research has shown it changes a young child's brain, is too distracting in and out of class, and kids need a time in their lives to be innocent and just be kids (not mini adults). It is estimated kids spend four to seven minutes a day outside, yet seven hours staring at a screen, not interacting with others. Is there something wrong with that for a developing young body?

The American Academy of Pediatrics recommends babies under 18 months avoid all screen media. Those 18-24 months can watch a little "quality" screen time with an adult watching with them. Those ages two to five should only watch screens an hour a day. For those ages 6+, the Academy recommends "media free meals" (talk instead), or take kids on drives. No child's bedroom should have a TV – too tempting and distracting from sleep. If this advice seems unrealistic, then make it a goal. Little kids should be exercising their limbs, not their eyeballs.

Adult Technology Issues

As whistleblower Edward Snowden pointed out in 2013, the NSA was spying on Americans, gathering private information, with phone companies violating Americans' privacy. Popular phone apps, including "Angry Birds," had collected info on the users, including location and personal demographics.

In 2020, privacy was starting to become important. By 2022, Google launched its own privacy labels for Google Play, with **some** ability to block ad tracking on Android devices. It is something kids and adults should both be worried about. So how much of your online data is private and safe, including a child's location? Investigate all your apps and find out.

It would seem like this is almost a battle, when to comes to young people and technology, an argument they are definitely losing. Nature, "human" nature, may be losing the battle, losing control of technology as it controls our youth. Maybe it's time all we all go outside for a walk and clear our heads. What do you think? The sandlot over TikTok? Time to decide.

Here are a few more tips to get our youth (and even some adults) away from technology, some of it suggested in Scott D. Sampson's book *How to Raise a Wild Child*. For the very young (preschool), take them outside. Let them splash in puddles when it rains and watch worms come out of the ground. Let them make mud pies and collect colored leaves to glue to paper and display for Halloween or Thanksgiving.

Older kids (ages 6-12+) need to be taken outside also—ask them to listen, smell, observe nature around your home or a nearby park. Emphasize its importance and talk about **your own interactions with nature.** Oh, what bird is that outside? Yep, red birds are cardinals. Where do they usually sit, in a tree near you? And if a group of birds suddenly goes quiet, did they leave? It could be a Cooper's hawk nearby they are afraid of. Oh, and do you smell those sweet roses? Did you notice that deer or groundhog? Where do you think they live? Could YOU easily live in the woods?

Yes, get young people outside, riding a bike, jumping rope, observing nature, and away from addicting electronic devices. Even camp in your backyard if you have one. Get them to exercise those young muscles, supervised and/or with a neighbor or friend their age. Encourage good mental health. The future will depend upon them one day!

Chapter Eight:
Artificial Intelligence (A. I.) and Robots –
Creepy or Essential?

In the TV series *Star Trek, Next Generation* (what can I say, I am sort of a Trekkie), one of the crew members enabled to help pilot the ship and make decisions about how to address hostile or new alien series is an android named Data. Lieutenant Commander Data is very calm and cool under pressure, and his pasty complexion gives away his designation. He is a robot, a robot who is self-aware enough to realize he has no emotions like his human companions. But he would like some. This is his fondest wish. He is a benign soul, a friendly male robot, one view of the future where A. I. is employed to create a whole new kind of being.

This is "one" view of robots. Another view is nasty, the scary looking terminator robots as seen in the *Terminator* movies from the 1980s and beyond. These robots are out for blood. These very human looking robots, in a wild, dystopian future, are programmed (and this is science fiction, folks) to "come back" to the past and kill the future child of one person, Sarah Conner. Her son John will be battling against these robots in the future because an A. I. defense system called Skynet wants to wipe out humanity, considering people a threat. That would never happen, right?

With robots, how can you tell? When did we get so hyped up about robots and A. I. anyway?

According to *Wired* magazine, the word "robot" appeared in 1921 in Czech Karel Capek's play "R.U.R.," or "Rossum's Universal Robots." Robot comes from the Czech word for "forced or manual labor," by the way. In the play, the robots go on a murdering spree. Capek later wrote to the *Oxford English Dictionary* that it was his brother Joseph who actually invented the term. In the 1940s sci-fi author Isaac Asimov invents the term "robotics," but it isn't till the early 1950s that George C. Devol of Louisville, Kentucky creates the earliest model of the modern robot. It was called Uninmate, for Universal Automation. Unfortunately, he couldn't get a company interested in his creation.

Later, Joseph Engelberger got Devol's patent and modified the model so it could become a useful, industrial robot. He designed one model called "Shaky." It wheeled around, not walking, had TV eyes, and was generally wobbly. Pictures of it make it look almost like an old projector on a set of metal drawers with wheels. By the mid-1980s the Honda company was making humanoid robots that could walk or shake hands. In 2014, then President Obama received a soccer ball kicked by a little *Asimo* robot.

There are other cute robots from Japan, like *PARO*, a robot that looks like a furry white seal, being used in nursing homes. There is also a robot that can lift the elderly like *Robear* or the robot *Hug.* According to the MIT Technology Review, it may be something Japan has been working on for decades because of an aging population, and not enough youth to replace it. But the robots have had to be vigorously promoted in order to get any acceptance.

It's been a bit of a novelty act, but robotics are used now in surgeries, car manufacturing, and other sectors of the economy. In my region they are even trying out (and hear Amazon will too in the near future) delivery of different items by drone, the little flying robots of today. It seems like fun and very innocent.

But robots are costing people jobs.

CNBC reports that robots could replace 20 million jobs by 2030, many in manufacturing. But making factories totally run by robots is not a given for total success. Tech whiz Elon Musk wanted his Tesla factory to be run TOTALLY by robots. He had predicted 20,000 cars a month would be made by the end of 2017. But he had to reverse course.

It was more like 2,425 were completed by robots for the last three months of 2017. He had to hire hundreds of human beings to help out.

And CHAT GPT may be helping students cheat. It is A. I. intelligence they can access over the internet, though it uses knowledge in its huge databanks from 2021. It is considered a "language bot" and Google and Microsoft are creating theirs as well. It has an ML algorithm with a simple starter text; it must predict the next word and so adjust its internal connections. It was trained with eight million web pages of knowledge and can create essays. For a <u>New York Times</u> column, some teenagers were asked about trying out ChatGPT and they said the essay answers were simplistic and would give them no incentive to research things. Some teens said it should be allowed.

Some adults say it is an unreliable tool. No one at this point has said anything about how much it would cost if say, you're a college student and have a 10 page paper due the next day. There are already some sites that help students write or edit a paper, with some listed on the <u>jasper.ai</u> site. It just goes to show that you can cheat if you want to, but if you are a mature, grown-up adult, would you want to?

The creepier issue, of course, is the issue of self-awareness, or being a sentient being. Could robots or robot systems ever become sentient? Just how complicated a process is it that our brain does every day?

Guilio Tononi, psychiatrist and neuroscientist at the University of Wisconsin, Madison, points out that any mechanism with intrinsic power, whose state is laden with its past and present and future, is conscious (which sounds a bit confusing). Consciousness has to do with being aware of your internal systems and external world. The mind uses different areas of the brain to recall a memory, like a birthday party where there would be smells, music, different colors, and it would all come together in the brain like connecting puzzle pieces. Could a robot really do that?

Physicist Stephen Hawking felt that A. I. in robots could one day make them superior in thinking to people, and then cause a threat (though it's logical to assume robots won't be coming from the past to help annihilate us). If warfare drones become *too* smart or robots built for warfare decide to switch sides, then that could be a problem.

It is more likely, like in author Kazuo Ishiguro's book *Klara and the Sun*, that small robots might be created to become companions. In the book a sick teen girl has a female robot companion because she has no siblings, and her mother thinks the robot could be a "replacement" if the daughter gets too ill and dies. Such a group of robots would take up a heck of a lot of resources. Why have a metal friend when you could have the real thing?

Where A. I. or scientific advancements could really come into their own is with enhancing the human body. The popular TV show *The Six Million Dollar Man* had an injured astronaut being rebuilt so that he has bionic (artificial) legs, a bionic arm and one bionic eye. We already have prosthetic arms we have connected to muscle and nerves so that just by thinking people can move them. Now an idea has been approved to try to help those who have suffered a stroke, injury, or Alzheimer's in the hippocampus, the part of the brain that deals with creating long term memory, personality, and behavior. It would use a computer chip to replace some of the hippocampus and integrate it in by bypassing lesions.

Biomedical engineer Theodore Berger with the University of Southern California is working on this memory idea, and he's already had some success with rats. But the human brain with its billions of neurons is much more complex, so experimenting and succeeding with giving humans a "memory prosthesis" is the next step. If this *does work*, could we be a lot closer to the so-called singularity, where robots are sentient, and then could we give them our memories to pass on to the next generation somehow?

Biotech businesswoman and United Therapeutics founder, Martine Rothblatt, claims she is already working on an android model, that looks like her wife Bina (BINA48). It is supported by artificial intelligence and talks, with chatbot help. Science fiction could become science fact in the future. And the ethics behind different actions are usually discussed after the fact. A. I. and computers' powers are a concern to some. Shouldn't we lay down some ground rules now? In this instance, technology could be winning in a hopefully beneficial way.

Chapter Nine:
Chemicals, Plastics (And What about the Ocean?)

It is said that hair dyeing has been around as far back as the time of Cleopatra (70 B.C. to 30 B.C.). They also used henna or other natural ingredients to dye cloth, the cloth being made from natural fibers like cotton, wool, linen (from flax), silk (from the silkworm). Over the last century or so we humans have turned to manmade, synthetic materials for most clothing. We have also manipulated other natural things, with food additives, certain ingredients in cosmetics, detergents for washing clothes, plastics and <u>polymers</u>, making things last longer.

Is bentonite with its softening benefits in a product like <u>Tide</u> laundry detergent something that washes out of your clothes, and is it healthy to be in contact with? Are all synthetic materials out there healthy?

It depends.

This writer was given an eyecare product (brand name <u>Systane</u>) that was basically all propylene glycol. Did you know that chemical has been used in shampoos, salad dressing, **and antifreeze**? I only put it in one eye. It was so irritating I couldn't sleep that night. I tossed it. (Play it safe and don't use that harsh chemical in your eyes.)

But we've grown used to having chemicals, many preservatives, in our lives – in our baked goods, other processed and packaged foods, yogurts, deli meats, even clothes you buy in the department store, with the recommendation you wash them one or two times before you even use them –the clothes, not the food. Why are we floating in so many chemicals?

Convenience. These chemicals are supposed to protect food quality, flavor, how long something stays on the shelf. After all, who likes mold? Chemicals make it happen. Chemicals have also given us vaccines, cancer treatments, computer screens, plastic. For centuries we depended on sugar and salt to preserve food. Now, <u>sodium benzoate</u> and calcium disodium EDTA preserve our baked goods or soda and are our chemical friends.

Oddly, calcium disodium EDTA is a considered both a food additive AND an ingredient in cosmetic and industrial products and detergent. The Food and Drug Administration (FDA) has set limits on the amount a food can contain. But the substance actually binds to excessive metals in the blood, in what they call chelation therapy. Research, as with many preservatives, is limited on whether it can cause cancer. But the source *Healthline* says researchers find it may disrupt the intestinal food barrier and be bad for inflammatory bowel disease. There is "mixed" animal study evidence it causes health problems.

Some have expressed concern about the amount of chemicals we Americans are exposed to. Organizations like the Environmental Working Group (<u>www.ewg.org</u>) have a database of some 20,000 (!) products and the chemicals that are in them. It has helpful recommendations for the least harmful, healthier, and even organic choices.

Laundry

Let's take a look at laundry detergents. They have chemicals called "surfactants" in them. The Human and Environmental Risk Assessment Initiative (HERA) conducted these risk assessments of several surfactants and found they "don't have a negative impact on the environment in their current uses." They are cleaning agents; they allow dirt to be removed from the surface of what is dirty, in combination with water. They are also added to car engine lubricants. Yes, it's true.

Some, though, believe that at high enough concentrations, they are toxic to animals and plants, and recommend a better choice. (See https://epa.gov/saferchoice/, or try detergents like Seventh Generation All Purpose Cleaner, or Honest Company Laundry Detergent.) The EWG also recommends Arm & Hammer Clean and Simple Detergent.

Even the National Library of Medicine (nebi.nlm.nih.gov) has published information on the "challenging issue" of surfactants as an "emerging contaminant," put in the environment through wastewater treatment. There is concern they could penetrate drinking water through said systems, especially anionic surfactants, but it is a complex issue. Down the line these chemicals could react with existing protein in the liver or cause respiratory issues. And we talking about not just one, but a class of chemicals.

The ever reliable *Consumer Reports* may report that Tide Plus Ultra Stain Release got third place in their tests for effective cleaner. But the U. S. Consumer Product Safety Commission says it's toxic because it also has the solvent 1,4-dioxane, which the U. S. EPA considers a likely human carcinogen, causing liver toxicity. Unfortunately, this is in most detergents, even the plant based Mrs. Meyers. (Check out the ewg.org database on that one.)

Toxicity **does depend** on how much you are exposed to an ingredient. Industrial and farm workers, in general, have some of the highest exposure to various chemicals.

Let's Look At Hair Dyes

Hair dyes have these surfactant "combining agents" too. The Naturtint brand doesn't have ammonia, which is harsh on your scalp. But one source claimed whatever chemical it did have may hurt the hair cuticle. Sometimes you just can't win. I personally try to not dye my hair too often; it is recommended you wash it the day before you dye it so it will hold the color longer, and not shampoo it after dyeing for at least a day.

Actually, Dr. Andrew Weil's *Self Healing* magazine (2020) refers to a study done by the U.S. National Institutes of Health, examining how hair dyes and straighteners affected some 40,000+ women. And they all had at least one sister with breast cancer. Black women who used permanent hair dyes every five to eight weeks had a 60 percent increased risk of having breast cancer. With white women, there was also an increased risk of breast cancer (also figuring in the genetic risk factor).

That's the thing. So-called "permanent" hair dyes, a misnomer because they **will** wash out in six to eight weeks, especially for dark shades, expose you to more harsh chemicals, more health risks. It is recommended to use "semi-permanent" dyes instead, such as the "Reflex Semi-permanent" hair color by <u>Naturtint</u>.

PFAs

What are really worrisome are per-and polyfluorinated alkyl substances – PFAs. They are considered "forever chemicals" that take, well, forever to break down in the environment. PFAs were found in the <u>Roanoke River</u> in Virginia in 2022. Unfortunately, PFAS are ALSO found in food packaging, nonstick cookware, clothing, cosmetics, and could cause kidney cancer, thyroid disease, liver damage, or developmental issues for a developing fetus (moms take note).

Although PFAs and perfluorooctanoic acid (PFOA) are no longer produced, they're still in the environment and accumulate in the body. (RTI International says it's working on testing to make PFA molecules disintegrate.) Let's hope it works. And soon.

Endocrine Disruptors

Artist Andy Warhol once said, "Everybody's plastic, but I love plastic." It's a little odd that plastic (which appears to be hard but mostly isn't) is also unhealthy, because it's everywhere. No doubt you've heard about BPA— or bisphenol A, which is in many plastic food containers, linings of canned vegetables and soup, for example. BPA is an estrogen mimicker, a xenoestrogen.

That's right. According to *Healthline*, since it appears to be like estrogen as it can bind to hormone receptors, and affect your reproductive system and thyroid. Too much in a woman's system could cause estrogen dominance, which could lead to a type of breast cancer.

If you choose BPA free products, you're helping your system. Plastics number 2, 4, and 5 are considered safest to recycle and no doubt use. Avoid numbers 1, 3, 6, and 7, but **all products will leach out chemicals**. A glass, ceramic, or stainless steel bottle or container is better to use, especially in the microwave oven.

PETE (Polyethylene Terephthalate, Number 1 plastic) is supposed to be used just once. Number 2 (HDPE) plastic is a high density ratio and can be used in various conditions, and is good for use in rope, toys, stools, bottles for cosmetics. No. 3 (polyvinyl chloride) is not safe. It's dangerous.

Of course, none of this is great in the ocean. When I taught logic, I had my students read about Capt. Charles Moore in Susan Casey's article "Plastic Ocean". Several years ago, he sailed to the doldrums, where the Pacific Ocean is calm, and came upon the Great <u>Pacific Garbage Patch</u>. This is a big area (actually two areas) the size of Texas, with lots of plastic debris.

Turtles, seabirds, seals, mistake this crap in the water for a sea creature like jellyfish they can eat. Plastic doesn't break down quickly – maybe in 500 years – so these sea animals are starving themselves and dying on this. We need to clean up the oceans. We need to clean up our plastic dependent lives. Take cloth bags to the supermarket, or demand stores use less and less plastic. In a Walmart in northern New York, they didn't hand out plastic bags.

It's a small start. We need to do more. Our world has just too darn much plastic and is too full of suspicious chemicals for our own good. Mother Earth is disappointed, I'm sure, with this technology. Plastics are too abundant and human and other life may be in a losing, unhealthy battle if we don't start producing less.

Chapter Ten:
Just a Few Words On the Pandemic

Recently, the United States and the rest of the world suffered through a very unhealthy period. A <u>pandemic</u> causes great illness or deaths, and this one took a while for a vaccine to be developed against the coronavirus, <u>COVID-19,</u> so that we could lead normal lives again. Leading up to the vaccine and beyond, governments put in place safeguards to protect people from this very serious illness.

Some thought this was **too much**.

Recently, U. S. Supreme Court justice Neil Gorsuch, a conservative appointee of former President Trump, said emergency measures taken during the COVID-19 epidemic-pandemic were "the greatest intrusions on civil liberties in the peacetime history of this country." Maybe so.

Did he logically look at all the reasons why there were restrictions on liberty during the COVID-19 pandemic?

Yes, we restricted kids going to school in person because, logically, rooms full of unvaccinated youth, whose vaccine didn't come in till much later, could spread a deadly virus for which there was then no cure/vaccine. Yes, there were prohibitions on evicting people because some people, especially in the hospitality industry, lost jobs or had to stay at home with their kids, causing them to be unable to pay the rent. Yes, we spent "way-too-much-time" on our computers at home. Couldn't we argue that this was all very necessary, though?

When you are fighting a type of Sars virus that has spread across the globe and thousands are dying because of it, some stringent health measures would logically reduce the number of sick people. Is wearing a mask in public and isolating those with a life threatening, contagious illness not a sensible thing to do? And if you have the "technology" to create a vaccine to save lives, shouldn't people take it, and not think of it as a **political thing** the government is forcing on you? Logically?

During COVID-19's pandemic my trip to Yellowstone was canceled by a bus company. But we **did go,** renting a car, in 2022, with COVID more under control – though people out West thought it was over and just about no one was wearing a mask that fall.

During 2020-2022, COVID -19 certainly had the upper hand. Now there are folks who early in the pandemic, especially, have suffered from long COVID symptoms. See https://www.cdc.gov/coronavirus/2019-ncov/long-term-effects/ index.html, which includes symptoms like chest pains, digestive issues, foggy brain, and more for many, many months.

Now the Biden administration (spring 2023) has officially ended the pandemic rules and restrictions. It's more up to us as individuals. If you are very young or old, have risk factors like diabetes or obesity, or being overweight even, you should continue to wear a mask in confined spaces in public. That's because some people have **still not gotten vaccinated.** The science proves that vaccines work.

And now Paxlovid has come out to help you even more. If you take it within five days of having COVID-19 symptoms (which include fever, body aches, cough, vomiting, diarrhea, weakness, headache, or a combination of these, after testing positive for the disease), Paxlovid will tremendously help lessen your symptoms and keep you out of the hospital. This writer contracted the virus at a big basketball game and taking Paxlovid helped some.

They say the coronavirus particles measure 120 nm (and a nanometer is one billionth of a meter). This tiny, nasty germ packs a big wallop and has killed millions. It would be wise to protect yourself from this nasty bug. COVID-19 can be a natural killer, but in this instance thank heaven we have the technology to hold it at bay.

Chapter Eleven:
Meditation: A Break From Electronics

In the debate that is "nature versus technology," sometimes we humans are both **quite overwhelmed** and really **used to having** technology in our lives, it seeming to take over (to win).

Maybe we are too "removed" from reality with these electronic devices, and spending oodles and oodles of hours on streaming apps/channels like Netflix, YouTube, TikTok dancing, Twitter/X comments, or even on the college based Desire2Learn platform.

How does one take a break from all this noise and distraction? Can your mind ever calm down and destress?

Yes. It's called "Mindfulness Meditation". Maybe some call it letting your mind go blank, zoning out, being peaceful (which is possible with some concentration). <u>Zen Buddhists</u> say, "Reduce, let go, leave (it) behind." They further say that you can have negative thoughts that they consider delusions. Modern society does little to reduce these delusions, like self-doubt and envy of others. Yes, modern society makes things difficult, but you can find a way out of this, dwelling on **the breath**.

Here are examples of mindfulness:
1) Paying attention to and concentrating on your breathing;
2) A body scan technique, where you pay close attention to physical sensations;
3) Learning to notice your thoughts.

In a 2020 Italian study, the three techniques above were used over eight weeks, which included a control group and a group who just read about the meditation techniques. At the end of the study, all three active groups increased their ability to be mindful and decreased rumination, the latter a repetitive, negative pattern of thought that is linked to depression. The participants all developed a more positive view of the future. They became more optimistic. Dr. Susanna Feruglio, Ph. D. student in psychology at Rome's Sapienza University, concurs that adjusting your conscious mind to shift attention away from inner thoughts, to breathing, will likely bolster optimism over time.

(A belief in God and attending weekly services can also make one more optimistic, and optimism can help the immune system.)

Here's an example of how to DO IT (for five to 20 minutes):

1) Sit on the floor or on the bed;
2) Close your eyes; slowly breathe;
3) Count your breaths; feel your diaphragm rising and falling;
4) If you want, cross your legs and lean your arms on them and connect index finger to thumb; have your mind only thinking about the breaths, and nothing else; feel peaceful.
5) After three/five to 20 minutes, you're done. Start your day, or do it later in the day when it is convenient. Work on being upbeat. It's a new day!

Chapter Twelve:
Guns, Mass Shootings, Shot Deer (Oh My)

Guns have been used to put a meal on the dining room table, to protect the family from intruders, for defense and offense in war. In modern times, some question their everyday need.

According to History.com, over a 1,000 years ago the Chinese were working on weapons. It was rather inadvertent, so to speak.

Back then there was a big interest in alchemy (and fireworks, invented in China about 200 B. C.). Alchemy was the Medieval interest in turning a chemical substance into gold, or creating an elixir to supposedly prolong life, or have immortality. In working on this idea, the Chinese discovered gunpowder, which was a black powder for a while. They found gunpowder was great for fireworks – *another thing* we got from Asia. Their weapon, though, consisted of a bamboo tube for a barrel.

Then Marco Polo and other explorers in the 13th century visited, and firearms soon spread across Europe. By the 15th century, the design had really improved. American colonists carried a simple "matchlock" weapon, which used a slow burning match to ignite the gunpowder in a barrel. In the 16th century the colonists used a musket, an on-the-shoulder device that used a flintlock to ignite the gunpowder. Then pistols, handheld guns, improved, with designs like the Colt 45 and the Luger, designed for accuracy and speed, and both defense and offense.

Of course, during wars, we developed the Gatling gun (developed by Richard Jordan Gatling during the Civil War, according to the Encyclopedia Britannica), the tank, the bomb, missile, drone, all used to hit a target, including people. Over the millennia, and certainly since World War II, guns of war have developed even more so. Faster, streamlined. The average U. S. citizen does not have legal access to a missile launcher, <u>drone</u> or (UCAV), tank, Gatling gun, or machine gun.

Then, the AK-47 came along.

The AK-47 is named after its inventor, Mikhail Kalashnikov, and was created for the Soviet military in 1947. It had certain advantages, such as a short barrel, curved magazine, the rapid fire of a machine gun, gas powered (yes, it pushes pistons), so that it can spit out 700 rounds a minute, according to <u>Popular Mechanics</u>.

Then an American company came up with something similar, the AR-15, in the 1950s, by Arma Lite Inc. This was a rifle popular with gun enthusiasts, with limited success as a military weapon. During the Vietnam war the M-16 was developed by the Colt company, which then went on to develop a semi-automatic version of it, also called the AR-15. After the Colt's patent ran out in the 1970s, other versions of the AR-15 came out, which begs the question of whether the average Joe needs this type of weapon out on the streets.

This question is asked because now it is the weapon of choice of mass shooters in America.

So what's with mass shooters and these semi-automatic assault rifles?

They can easily kill a group of people quickly in a short time. Rather than a pistol or a shotgun, they kill way <u>too many people</u> in a bloody fashion. Some judges are deeming these "weapons of war" as they can hurt so many.

The National Rifle Association (NRA) and other pro-gun groups say Second Amendment rights entitle them to use such a gun. Mothers Demand Action (MDA) and other parents of schoolchildren condemn the AR-15. It is easy to obtain, easy to take out a lot of people. Kids are

not deer in the woods. Even *Dick's Sporting Goods* wants to no longer sell these guns.

Mass shootings (sometimes a monthly thing) have taken a toll on the American psyche. No one wants their child to go to school in fear of being shot by a mentally disturbed (mostly young, mostly white) teen. Why can't these guys just talk to somebody?

Many have been bullied, are loners, and collect guns the way little girls collect Barbie dolls. Some decide to go out in a frightening blaze of glory. Why the heck doesn't this happen in England, say, or Japan?

In **those** countries, they understand guns are one technology it is better not everyone have. In England, even the average cop doesn't have a handgun. (I was acquainted with one who explained that when a group of drunks came toward him he hit them with pepper spray and ran for it.) And in Japan, you have to take a test every three years to keep your gun, safety being paramount.

In America, do you have to take a test, have a license, or be given a case to separate the gun from the bullets in the house in order to keep it from a child's hands? Good question.

One of the latest mass shooters, a Texas teen, had just turned 18. Salvador Ramos walked into a shop, and bought an AR-15 like it was candy. Then he went over to Robb Elementary in Uvalde, got in a back door, and shot 21 people to death. He treated them like deer in the woods. But deer that are shot get eaten. This was pointless. This is why these assault weapons were banned for civilians in the past (1994-2004). They could be again.

Some hunters argue AR-15s need to be available to them. But fewer and fewer people in the United States are actually hunting. The North Carolina College of Natural Resources has studied the numbers. In 1982 the numbers peaked, with 17 million hunters who purchased 28.3 million licenses.

Today (as of Jan. 2021), 11 million in the U. S. hunted, less than four percent of the population. And aging baby boomers (born 1949-1964) are a third of all hunters, aging right out of hunting.

Lincoln Larson, Professor of Parks, Recreation, and Tourism at North Carolina State College of Natural Resources, says hunting is fading. That is, ironically, bad for conservation. These sports licenses pay for animal conservation efforts, and the country's growing minority doesn't hunt much. Statistically, it's predicted whites will be just half the population by 2044.

What to do? Can this be solved?

Larson says there is some research into developing a program to target "nontraditional" hunters. As for funding, there is hope if the "Recovery Awareness Wildlife Act" (RAWA) becomes law, to provide $11.4 billion for fish and wildlife conservation. (As of January 2023, it did not become law.) There are a number of species in the U. S. that are endangered, from the Florida panther to the black-footed ferret, the Florida manatee to the Hawai'ian monk seal, and conservation would help them survive.

If there are a lot less hunters out there, do we **really need all these weapons** floating around?

Effect On Children

Once again, we need look at the effect of a certain technology on kids, kids not taught to hunt and respect nature (or even human life). Technology seems to be winning here. In John Woodrow Cox's book *Children Under Fire*, if there is a gun in the home it increases the risk of suicide threefold, according to David Hemenway, Director of the Harvard Injury Control Research Center, who feels gun violence is a **national health crisis.**

Children are also curious. In Cox's book, a survey of families in the South found 40 percent of parents who claimed their kids didn't know where their guns were stored were wrong (on page 304).

And should parents be held responsible for taking guns from said parents' home by kids? Only in Michigan, and now, Newport News, Virginia, where <u>a six year old shot</u> and seriously wounded his first grade teacher, have there been consequences for the actions of their kids, with the parents required to serve jail time.

Do parents and children both need instruction on gun safety? Should kids sign something like a pledge in school, that they will **not bring a weapon to school**, but will seek emotional support if they are hurting physically or emotionally? Logically, if we don't want technology to triumph in a negative way, this would be a first step.

Chapter Thirteen:
Climate Change

Where my middle son Adam lives, in Dallas, Texas, summers are normally hot. He once told me he took walks in the evening when things cooled down – at 90o F out! But now Mother Nature is really challenging the norm and our ability to cope. Phoenix, Arizona registered temps in the three digits (like 110+o F, or 43.3+ Celsius) over a month during the summer of 2023. Who can endure such constant high numbers? What are we living in, Iraq or something?

No, we're in the U. S., not Iraq. And there normally aren't tornadoes in Kentucky or fires in Hawai'i. Or Canada. We're in what some scientists call the <u>Anthropocene age</u>, an age where **people** (human beings) are causing the rise in global temperatures to abnormally high levels with their use of <u>fossil fuels</u>, fuels that will run out in the not too distant future (<u>perhaps in 50 years</u>, not taking Artic oil drilling into account).

Shall we blame industrialization? The Brits with their factories, replacing individual craftsmen and weavers, starting in the <u>1760s</u>? They didn't help, did they? Our modern conveniences, our cars, refrigerators, silverware, Jello pudding cups, TV dinners and more, require factories, factories that have produced CO2 emissions for many, many decades. Now, the earth is a hot mess.

What is Climate Change (Global Warming)?

So why is it such a big deal to have carbon dioxide in our atmosphere? Although we do also have oxygen and nitrogen in the air, they don't heat up the planet like CO2, and to a lesser extent, natural gas. When the sun's rays hit the earth's surface, it absorbs some of that energy, which it re-radiates as infrared waves that we feel as heat. Oxygen and nitrogen have only a few atoms each. CO2 has more (3+)

atoms and absorbs energy at a wavelength of 2,000- 15,000 nanometers, which is an overlap with infrared energy; CO2 then "soaks it up" and re-emits it in all directions, half into space and half to the earth as heat, the so-called greenhouse effect. (The <u>greenhouse effect</u> also includes the gases methane, nitrous oxide, chlorofluorocarbons or halogens, such as <u>freon</u>, and water vapor.)

Interesting note: The planet Venus is so full of vapor in its atmosphere that it's not as hot as our planet will be in the future if climate change continues, by one estimate. But that idea could be off, as it is now 700+ degrees Fahrenheit (370+ Celsius) on the Venus surface.

Why care about our planet?

A few years ago environmental activist Bill McKibben got together with some friends and founded 350. Their website, 350.org, makes it clear that we are in a race against time.

Their authority, Dr. James Hansen, Columbia University physicist directing the Program on Climate Science, says, "If humanity wished to preserve the planet similar to that on which civilization developed [and] to which life on Earth is adapted, paleoclimate evidence and ongoing climate change suggest that CO2 will need to be reduced from [current levels] to at most, 350 ppm." In other words, having more than 350 parts per million of carbon atoms in our atmosphere threatens the survival of living things on this planet.

But <u>www.mn350.org</u> says we are "already" at 400+ ppm of CO2 in the <u>atmosphere</u>. And you can see the results of that, with droughts leading to recent fires in California, Canada, even Hawai'i and Texas. Canadian fire smoke even drifted down into the States as far as Virginia in 2023.

In 2021, we were at 1.1 degrees Celsius (33.98 degrees Fahrenheit) above preindustrial warming temps, because carbon emissions to the atmosphere had increased. Many in the science world are concerned. Scientists now predict that at 1.5 degrees Celsius, 70-90 percent of coral reefs in the world will die, as reported by NPR. At 2 degrees C of warming above preindustrial levels, 99 percent will be lost and affect the 500 million people out there who depend on the marine ecosystem for their livelihoods. Therefore, millions would starve.

At current rates we will be on track to hit 1.5 degrees Celsius of warming above preindustrial temps by the end of this decade. It is a perilous time many governments and businesses are ignoring. Current U.S. President Joe Biden revoked one oil pipeline permit, which TC Energy abandoned on June 2, 2021. Biden also helped pass bills to improve the country's infrastructure and promote green energy products. He plans to buy carbon neutral electricity or work toward it, signing an executive order to cut government carbon emissions 65 percent by 2030.

Even though his goal is to cut government CO2 emissions to "net zero" by 2050, he is not consistent. He has to work with pro-business Republicans. So he's **also approved** more oil and gas permits on federal lands.

Of course, by economic sector, China is producing the most climate warming gases, at 30 percent (Feb. 2023), according to the United States Environmental Protection Agency (EPA). In 2020, *Forbes* reported that over 15 percent of China's energy would be from non-fossil fuel sources. Some would deem that number rather low.

Currently (September 3, 2023), Bloomberg News has reported that a major China coal producer, Shenhua Energy, intends to build more (what?!) plants to meet energy needs. China has also "vowed" to reduce fossil fuel emissions by 2030, at the latest. Is anyone listening to climate scientists **now?**

According to statista.com, coal is meeting under 25 percent of energy needs in the U. S. (2023), thanks in part to environmental groups like the <u>Sierra Club</u> pushing to close coal burning plants. Natural gas has replaced some plants because it's gotten cheaper. Yet it also contributes to climate change, and may affect the atmosphere more in the short run, while <u>dissipating</u> a lot quicker than CO2. It is no wonder Virginia activists are **still protesting** the Mountain Valley Pipeline's (MVP) completion and operation.

The MVP is also an experiment. There's never been a natural gas pipeline 42 inches in diameter, going through <u>mountainous</u>, karst topography. The project's been cited for hundreds of <u>environmental</u> violations like erosion and sedimentation of streams, and endangering some fish and bat species. After five plus years of work, the pipeline is completed, and is still violating EPA standards.

Also affecting the atmosphere? That daggone war with Ukraine, or any current wars. Some claim Ukraine's war with Russia has been a "climate disaster," of its own, with disruption of oil and natural gas supplies to Europe, with missiles and explosions creating the equivalent of 120 million metric tons of planet heating pollution in one year alone.

It is obvious individuals, governments, and businesses need to work together to lower climate change emissions— chlorofluorocarbons, methane (natural gas), carbon dioxide, and nitrous oxide. In order for there to be any kind of sustainable, healthy future for Mother Earth and us, we must bear responsibility for this and cut emissions **now**. Our technology created this problem and our technology needs to fix this. (CO2 is coming from our technology, hurting us with crazy weather up in the troposphere, where most of it stays.)

Chapter Fourteen:
Conclusions (And Some Solutions)

Well – thought about all of this enough?

There are many ways to look at the issues revolving around technology and its effect on nature (human OR Mother Nature related).

For example…

When we went on a recent trip, we "tried" to get one of those timers you plug in and connect to your lamp to come on at night (or during the day, or any time) while we were away. The directions provided no help when followed. It didn't work. Sometimes technology is like that. Not too helpful. Actually, it sort of worked. We left it on and after arriving home found it had turned itself off!

Guns – With Kids or Anyone

Take guns. In the nature vs. technology debate, it would seem, at least in the United States, that guns have such a foothold in our culture's thinking that humans seem overwhelmed, not in control, losing the battle. In 2022 alone, there were mass school shootings, and <u>shootings</u> out in public, every month, sometimes every week!

There are those who say those semi-automatic assault weapons, the weapons of choice for mass murder, currently the AR-15, need to be available because of our <u>Second Amendment</u> rights to bear arms. Current access to guns is making schools unsafe. And more children suffer.

Those in favor of AR-15 access are not thinking about the future, specifically the kids. Why would we encourage this? Why have access to bump stocks and multi-magazine bullet clips, the former the federal

court lifted a ban on in early 2023? (See
https://www.cnn.com/2023/01/06/politics/bump-stocks-guns-appeals-court/index.html.)

If you want protection, a handgun, with bullets in a separate area if there are kids in the house, would make more sense.

As for kids in schools, there should not only be mental health classes, but all grades, 1-12, should do a "pledge" on paper, to let them know guns and weapons in schools are NOT the solution to your problems. This author even wrote about this in the *Roanoke Times.* In October 2007, there was a "Day of National Concern about Young People and Gun Violence." With that came a student pledge to not bring weapons to school.

See www.pledge.org, where you can download a pledge for younger students (grades 1-5) and older pupils. You can get more info at: Student Pledge Against Gun Violence, 112 Nevada Street, Northfield, Minnesota 55057.

Though the current U. S. Supreme Court (2022) said you have a right to bear arms in public for self-defense, till we make assault weapons, multi-magazine clips, ghost guns less available/unavailable to our unhappy youth, mass shootings (including mass school shootings) will continue. In the gun debate, the "guns" seem to be winning.

AI

It looks like AI (artificial intelligence) is going to be with us for, probably, forever now. Astrophysicist Neil deGrasse Tyson believes AI can "crunch the numbers" with boring data from outer space. Physicist Stephen Hawking felt AI could be very helpful to mankind.

But Hawking also warned that it could "bypass us" and lead to our doom. Too pessimistic? If we program AI to be incredibly logical, it *could* look at our wars, our environmental degradation, the big threat that is climate change, or nuclear war, and think, wouldn't the earth be better off without humans?

Business and government leaders are now looking at how to regulate AI to keep it from overrunning our systems. An IT servers provider "Insight" survey has found business leaders anticipate using "generative AI" (such as ChatGPT) in the future for:
- employee productivity (72%);
- customer service (66%);
- research and development (53%).

Microsoft cofounder Bill Gates worries AI generated computer code could search for software vulnerabilities needed to hack computers; he'd like to see a regulatory agency formed that is similar to that of the International Atomic Energy Agency. He believes that in the future the "deepfakes" (faces and voices) people will get better at identifying online. MIT (Massachusetts Institute of Technology) actually has info on how to identify a deepfake online at: https://www.media.mit.edu/projects/detect-fakes/overview/.

So—is AI going to hurt us, especially if it is put in some futuristic robot? So far, "human" nature has control and "seems" to be winning the argument on this one, though some artists and writers may disagree.

Smartphones and Computer Screens

When it comes to so-called smartphones, this technology is really invading the lives of children/teens. Those under 40 seem very much "in need" of that constant presence, though parents are partly to blame for sticking these devices into their hands at a very young age.

A landmark study by the National Institutes of Health has found kids who spend more than two hours a day looking at a screen got lower scores on thinking and language tests. Young students on smartphones are not biking, going outside, or getting enough sleep, the last due to blue light screen exposure. Richard Louv's book *Last Child in the Woods: Saving Our Children from Nature Deficit Disorder* was written in 2007, and is even **more appropriate** for parents and guardians to follow now.

That's because if kids are outside, they are less likely to be cyber bullied over the phone/computer screen. Smartphones are a very persuasive, pervasive thing. In this area, we humans are not winning.

As mentioned already, we can do better with encouraging and having kids get involved with other activities like sports, drawing, playing board games, seeing and talking to others in person. Parents can set an example and **not live on the smartphone** or be a helicopter parent and text kids while in school. In Los Angeles and <u>Montgomery County</u>, Virginia, there are even plans to ban kids from most smartphone use in school. The federal government is also looking at <u>regulating ads</u> influencing kids online.

There **are many other things to do** besides looking at Facebook, TikTok, YouTube, Instagram. Reclaim conversation at the coffee shop, club meeting, community dance, dinner table.

CARS

Cars and transportation have unique possibilities and could prove to be neutral in the nature vs. technology argument. Since we love our cars and refuse to get rid of them, let's make as many electric and hybrid cars as we can. Close to thirty percent of U. S. carbon <u>emissions the EPA</u> says come from transportation: planes, trains, buses, jets, trucks, and, of course, cars. **All** sectors need to become more fuel efficient and pollute the air less to help a heating planet.

We **can** push the government to make the Big Three automakers (Ford, General Motors, Chrysler/Stellantis) build and promote smaller cars, not SUV tanks—<u>SUVs</u> are responsible for many vehicle accidents or deaths with pedestrians, by the way. We can also drive less, carpool, bike, and keep our cars in tiptop working order to add less C02 to the environment.

One interesting thing in transport – Ohio, where the Wright brothers worked on the first planes, is where work is being done on an electric plane (!) of sorts. Joby Aviation, based in California, is planning to locate its first manufacturing facility at the Dayton International Airport. Worldwide, electric vertical takeoff and landing (eVTOL) is becoming a "thing". This air vehicle would become an "air taxi" for four people, put in a ridesharing network by 2025. It's not electric jets (we need faster work done on hydrogen cell technology for that, 20 years away), but is a unique concept we could explore more.

Now there is also a singular, electric flying vehicle called the "Jetson ONE" being sold, for a cool $98,000. It will have little spinning blades like a helicopter and be able to go up over 1,000 feet and do a 20 minute ride. Anything to help reduce our <u>carbon footprint</u>.

Food

Food actually relates to climate change and could help us all. I recently attended a program on <u>biochar</u>, an old method of enhancing soil ingredients and producing better crop yields. Any <u>regenerative agriculture</u>, or organic agriculture helps the planet and people too. Yes, buying organic can provide you with more nutrients, and less synthetic chemicals like pesticides, and is healthier for your <u>immune system</u> too.

Plastics—Ocean—Chemicals

Chemicals make it happen, for good or ill. Chemicals have benefited humankind since the Pharaohs of Egypt decided to be mummified, using products like bitumen, beeswax, plant oils like castor oil and pistachio oil, the last two just for the head.

We have pumped oil from the ground to give us gasoline and plastics, a gasoline byproduct. Chemicals, including preservatives, used in our food, clothes, medicines, and even coal burning plants, may have as many side effects as benefits. It is recommended if you are concerned about your cosmetics to check the big database of chemicals at the Environmental Working Group site: www.ewg.org. The ewg.org also has information on safer materials for consumers.

But plastics, including microplastics and nurdles (plastic pellets less than 5 mm big), are still **all over, even <u>in our blood</u>**. Not great.

When the spouse and I visited N. Y. State (July 2023), the local Walmart would not give out plastic bags. The employees would take your purchase to the car, with no plastic bag in sight. So some people are trying to cut plastic waste.

At age 16, in 2011, Dutchman <u>Boyan Slat</u> found **more plastic than fish** when he went scuba diving during a trip to Greece. It was unsettling, to say the least. He was inspired to create a device to collect plastic garbage at sea. He's now CEO of The Ocean Cleanup Initiative, with plans to remove 80 percent of the plastic at sea by 2030, 90 percent by 2040. He promised to do that in a letter to the U. N. Ocean Conference.

His system uses a kind of moving dam carried by two boats, the currents helping to push it toward a net that closes and is taken to a boat to unload. Boyan Slat's idea is effective and needed, and he's gotten awards for this. Yes, we don't want to eat plastic. We are overwhelmed by this junk in our environment. Don't let plastic win the argument. Recycle, reuse, use less, including carrying around cloth bags.

Our Worse Crisis – Climate Change

Picture if you will, a city, on fire. Literally. There are flames coming out of tall buildings, only blocks from the ocean, and, snared in traffic, are families frantically beeping horns and yelling out windows at the car in front of them, flames on dry land only a few feet from the roadway.

Suddenly, the fire roars across cars with those families, who are desperately trying to escape their vehicles so they can run to the edge of the road and into the ocean several feet below. It's a regular heat Armageddon. The only thing missing from this horror picture is a giant alien from outer space controlling the whole scene.

This isn't some dystopian scene from *The Twilight Zone* TV show. It's real life, and 101 people died in this horror in Lahaina, Hawai'i (August 2023).

Some of the calls to 9-1-1 were kept for posterity and are heart rending. After spraying his house with water one man told 911, "I don't know if we can get out." He was surrounded by a fire and brimstone environment. One woman pleaded, "I cannot get out of my door – there's flames blowing into the house! I have a baby!"

While we continue to debate if climate change is real, people are dying. We need to take better care of the environment. It is interesting to note that at one time there were half a million bison living in the United States, when Native American tribes roamed the land. There was a balance between humans and nature, very unlike now.

In the nature vs. technology debate, Mother Nature seems to be winning overall, but actually, all this heat is even making her sick, the melting ice caps warming the oceans and creating crazy weather patterns. Climate change shows our lack of control over nature because of our harmful technology (fossil fuel emissions). It is threatening the animal/insect kingdom and our way of life.

No matter what your political party is, climate change is not some fad. It's here and not going away. You have only to watch the movie <u>*Chasing Ice*</u> to recognize that the Artic ice cap and other places with glaciers are vanishing. Polar bears are running out of ice to hunt on.

According to the "Vital Signs" website, over the next 20 years, methane gases released today will 80 times more potent than climate warming from an equal amount of C02, says researcher Tianyi Sun. We need to therefore reduce both methane/natural gas AND carbon dioxide. If we just capped the one million abandoned oil/natural gas wells in the United States, it would make a meaningful methane reduction. But time is running out to get climate change under control **before we have no control over it at all.** Some say, in as little as six years it could be out of control:

(See https://www.livescience.com/planet-earth/climate-change/the-safe-threshold-for-global-warming-will-be-passed-in-just-6-years-scientists-say.)

The U. S., India, and China need to step up. America is somewhat responsible, because we are the energy and resource hog of the planet. India and China have burgeoning economies with almost half the earth's population, at almost three billion people. They also have a responsibility when it comes to emissions. We need to set green energy goals in the next few years and stick to them. Not climate change, but change the climate!

How Close Are We To An Ominous Future

The Columbia University Climate School article (Nov. 2021 online) "How Close are we to Climate Tipping Points" is talking the numbers.

The Intergovernmental Panel on Climate Change (IPCC) has warned that if we reach 2 degrees Celsius (35.6 degrees Fahrenheit) of warming above preindustrial levels there could be "catastrophic consequences" for the planet. IPCC estimates the tipping point of "no return" could be between 1o C and 2 o C of warming. We've already passed the 350 ppm (parts per million) of carbon dioxide and are now at 400+ ppm. Some predict if we reach 500 ppm we could reach the point where weather will just get worse and worse (because CO2 stays up in the atmosphere for many, many years).

The Transient Climate Response estimate is that at 1.5o Celsius we'd be at about 507 ppm and 2.0o C would be about 618 ppm. We're so close, but there are variables with weather patterns and we can STILL do things to mitigate or lessen the damage.

Besides what's already been mentioned (and it's been mentioned before), we in the States can drive small cars and less often. We can push legislators to make Exxon (maybe even refuse to buy their gas) to cap those abandoned wells and turn to renewables for states' utility companies nationwide. Tell those company shareholders this is about survival more than profits. We can continue to retire coal burning plants and go to solar/wave/offshore <u>wind projects,</u> the last being pursued in Virginia.

Take Politics Out and Make Sustainability A Thing

Native peoples, whether in America or elsewhere, had little or no technology. They depended on Mother Earth to take care of them so they had to live sustainably, not pollute, overfish, kill off all the bison and other animals they depended on. They were close to the land. They would say a prayer over the animal they killed for food. They were grateful to the planet. I have seen how conservation has helped the bison, for example, rebound and roam in herds at the wondrous Yellowstone National Park.

On the other hand, we modern humans just take and take from Mother Earth. We run around to manmade jobs and don't take time to smell the roses. In Japan, there is something called <u>Shinrin yoku,</u> or forest bathing. It is about calming walking in the woods, taking in nature, relaxing in nature. Being a part of Mother Earth. We need to do this, appreciate the woods, get in touch with nature, then learn about saving the resources we depend on, including our planet.

Yes, we need sustainability now, so that we can "change climate" now. Why is there not, for example, a Sustainability Index? There is actually something called the "<u>Environmental Sustainability Index,</u>"

but this is not mandated or required reading, or a required goal. That is really flawed. We need to make sustainability part of our national conversation, in America and elsewhere. We need a "sustainability index" up there with the Nasdaq and Wall Street numbers.

Perhaps we could make it a yearly contest, administered by local groups and a national **Sustainability Council**. This council would be responsible for getting the Big 3 (in autos, oil, countries with high output of carbon emissions) together to make pledges or follow laws set down by the government to get us "away" from 1.5 or 2.0 degrees Celsius. Otherwise, it could get so hot South Americans could be clambering at our border to get in. And if we "overwarm" the oceans and the phytoplankton start to die, then what oxygen will we have to breathe?

The Biden administration has been encouraged to put into action 10 priorities to address climate change. (See https://www.wri.org/insights/top-10-priorities-president-biden-tackle-climate-crisis.) The funny thing is, with politicians, **no one wants to talk about climate change**. Even in an election year!

There are things U. S. (even world) citizens can do now, including pushing their elected representatives to get a sustainability council going. (See https://coolclimate.org/calculator.)

Climate change, more than other technologies or conditions, should be considered our greatest threat to the future of a currently livable planet. As Washington Governor Jay Inslee says, "We're the first generation to feel the impacts of climate change and the last generation that can do something about it."

(See sources and resources after a short chapter on current "Updates".)

Chapter Fifteen:
Just a Few Updates

The most recent event related to gun use and kids, was the April (2024) conviction of Jennifer and James Crumbley in Michigan, of involuntary manslaughter. School officials wanted them to take son Ethan home after they noticed his dangerous drawing and written plea for help. These parents refused. Ethan took a handgun out of his backpack and killed four classmates with it. He's been given a life sentence, his parents sentenced to 10-15 years in jail.

The handgun had been a present. Couldn't they have given him one of those RPG video games or gone on a hike? Handguns and male teens don't mix, especially when they avoid talking about mental health issues and their parents give them easy access to a loaded gun.

AI and Online Regs

As this is being written, the U. S. Congress is working to regulate AI more directly in the future. Currently (May 2024), Congress has decided that with apps/sites like Facebook, Instagram, X (Formerly Twitter) and the like, they can regulate their own behavior. Come this fall, politicians can have a "field day" making up stuff to put on the internet. Concerned citizens "could" go learn what's what at nonpartisan sites like www.politifact.com or https://www.factcheck.org, to see how accurate information is that politicians or their supporters are presenting.

Helping the Climate!

Billionaire businessman Bill Gates, according to *The Guardian* online, (See https://www.theguardian.com/environment/2018/feb/04/carbon-emissions-negative-emissions-technologies-capture-storage-bill-gates.)

is supporting a startup company that would pull many tons of CO2 out of the atmosphere through a special photosynthetic process. Then this carbon neutral "fuel" could be used for the world's ships, trucks, or planes. This would be truly revolutionary and the world needs this to succeed.

Even as this is read, the ocean's coral reefs are being bleached, and if they die people on the planet depending on marine life could be in big trouble. *The Nature Conservancy* organization is working to grow more heat resistant strains of coral. Will this help enough to ensure the ocean's survival?

Much depends in the next five years on what we humans do to help the planet, so that the technology that produced so much carbon dioxide and methane does **NOT** win.

See some sources after the references and some continuing tips to help our planet and our health as well at: https://www.writerdjmathews.com/s-t-p/.

(Most) References

Abrams, S. (2013, May 16). *Vehicles have changed a lot. Their fuel? Not so much*. Retrieved July 26, 2022 from https://roadandtrack.com/car-culture/a445/the-road-ahead-fuel-evolution
https://climatehero.me

Cox, J. W. (2021). *Children Under Fire: An American Crisis*. Ecco.

Graber, D. (2019). *Raising Humans in a Digital World: Helping Kids Build a Healthy Relationship with Technology*. Harper Collins.

Hays, B. (2015). Ocean acidification will affect balance of plankton species. *Science News*. Retrieved October 11, 2023 from https://www.upi.com/Science_News/2015/07/22/ocean-acidification-will-affect-balance-of-plankton-species/8671437575762/

Hsaio, J. (2015, August 10). *GMOs and Pesticides: Helpful or Harmful?* Harvard University Graduate School of Arts and Sciences. Retrieved July 25, 2023 from https://sitn.hms.harvard.edu/flash/2015/gmos-and-pesticides/

Johnson, G., Lauer, C., Boone, R., & McAvoy, A. (2023, October 16). Maui fire 911 calls reveal terror, panic. *The Roanoke Times*, B7.

Kamin, D. (2023, October 5). Maybe in Your Lifetime, People Will Live on the Moon and Then Mars. *New York Times*. https://www.nytimes.com/2023/10/01/realestate/nasa-homes-moon-3-d-printing.html

MacDonald, L. (2014, August 5). *Reasons to Avoid Aspartame At All Costs*. activebeat. https://activebeat.com/diet-nutrition/10-reasons-to-avoid-aspartame-at-all-costs/2/

Perrigo, B. (2018, September 7). A Dutch Teenage had a dream to clean up the World's Oceans. 7 Years on, it's coming true. *Time*. Boyan Slat: Dutch Inventor To Launch Ocean Plastic Cleanup | Time

Ruggiero, G. (2023, Fall). The Risky Rise of AI. *Yes!* (107), 64-65.

Sampson, S. D. (2016). *How to Raise A Wild Child: The Art and Science of Falling in Love with Nature*. Mariner Books. Reprint Ed.

Shulman, L. (2022, August 24). Phones in my classroom have me worried about the future [Editorial]. *The Roanoke Times*, A8.

Stonor, C. (2023, September 21). Jetson One: Personal Flying Vehicle Sold Out For 2023, Nearly all of 2024. *eVTOL insights*. Retrieved November 7, 2023 from https://evtolinsights.com/2023/09/jetson-one-personal-flying-vehicle-sold-out-for-2023-nearly-all-of-2024/

Symons, A. (2023, January 2). Exxon makes record £51 billion profit. Only 5% is going to 'low carbon' projects. *Euro News*. https://www.euronews.com/green/2023/02/01/exxon-makes-record-51-billion-profit-only-5-is-going-to-low-carbon-projects

Smyth, J. C. (2023, September 21). Ohio makes deal with flying-taxi-Company. *The Roanoke Times*, B9.

Suderman, A., & Goodman, J. (2021, October 21). Amid riot, Facebook faced own insurrection. *The Roanoke Times*, B14.

Turkle, S. (2015). *Reclaiming Conversation: The Power of Talk in The Digital Age*. Penguin Press. 350.org. (2023). *Who We Are*. https://350.org/about

The Nature Conservancy. (2023, Winter). Natural Solutions to the Climate Crisis. *Nature Conservancy Magazine*, 7.

Resources
(Learn More/Join/Help out)

Brandes, H. (2023, September/October). Ecuador's Gold: Can the Most Coveted Chocolate in History help revive the forests around the World. *Smithsonian*, 54(04), 76-85.

Center for Science in the Public Interest. (2021). 10 Superstars…For Better Health! *Nutrition Action Newsletter.* www.endplasticwaste.org

Heid, M. (2014, October). Diet soda and cancer – What you should know. *The University of Texas MD Anderson Center.* https://www.mdanderson.org/_publications/focused-on-health/does-diet-soda-cause-cancer.h19-1589046.html

HT Correspondent. (2023, November 5). Government should step in to help businesses in efforts for sustainability: Abhyuday Jindal. *Hindustan Times.* Retrieved November 5, 2023 from https://www.hindustantimes.com/business/govt-should-step-in-to-assist-businesses-in-efforts-for-sustainability-abhyuday-jindal-101699166790993.html

Jackson, M. Z. (2023). *No Miracles Needed: How Today's Technology Can Save Our Climate and Clean Our Air.* Cambridge University Press.

Johnson, A. E., & Wilkinson, K. K. (Eds.). (2021). *All We Can Save: Truth, Courage, and Solutions for the Climate Crisis.* One World Trade Paperback.

Lent, J. (2021, Spring). Toward an Ecological Civilization. *Yes!* www.yesmagazine.com

Louv, R. (2019). *Our Wild Calling: How Connecting with Animals can Transform our lives – and save theirs*. Algonquin Books.

Pringle, L. (1981). *What Shall We Do with the Land: Choices for America*. Thomas Crowell.
https://www.sierraclub.org/climate-and-energy

United Nations Climate Change. (2023). *The Paris Agreement*.
https://unfccc.int/process-and-meetings/the-paris-agreement

Home - Waterkeeper

Van Noy, R. (2020). *Sudden Spring: Stories of Adaptation in a Climate-Changed South*. University of Georgia Press.

About the Author

Ms. D. J. Mathews has been a freelance writer, adjunct professor, and Master naturalist member, the last for the New River Valley Chapter in Virginia. She has written for such publications as the *Virginia Journal of Education, The Roanoke Times, Bristol Herald Courier*, and *Appalachian Trailway News*. Her past books include *Let's Run Our Schools Together* and the YA book *Great American Women in Science and Environment*. See more of her writing at www.writerdjmathews.com/blog/ and https://medium.com/@djmathews. She is also on Facebook and LinkedIn.com, and https://ko-fi.com/dj50772 . She is married and hails from Virginia.

www.ingramcontent.com/pod-product-compliance
Lightning Source LLC
Chambersburg PA
CBHW051215250726
48655CB00006B/2427